easy
SHEET
PAN MEALS

The Genius *Sheet Pan*

The recipes in this book were tested using a 13x18x1" half sheet pan. Smaller pans may not be large enough to accommodate these recipes.

Using a pan with lower 1" sides allows air to circulate around the food, roasting rather than steaming the ingredients. A pan without sides is a no-no for these recipes.

A good-quality heavy-duty pan will support hefty meals and won't warp from the heat of the oven.

Make sure your cupboard includes at least one sheet pan...
It just might become the most-used pan in your kitchen!

ISBN-13: 978-1-56383-647-3
Item #7157

Printed in the USA

Distributed By:

PO Box 850
Waverly, IA 50677

www.cqbookstore.com

gifts@cqbookstore.com

 CQ Products

 CQ Products

 @cqproducts

 @cqproducts

Keep it Clean

We suggest greasing your pan or lining it with aluminum foil or parchment paper for easy cleanup *(never use waxed paper)*. Many manufacturers recommend not using cooking spray.

If you really enjoy scrubbing dirty pans though, try this for getting them clean:

- In your sink, mix **½ C. baking soda** and **½ C. white distilled vinegar** *(it's going to fizz and bubble)*. Add **hot water**, then submerge your dirty pan in the concoction and soak at least an hour or up to overnight. If your sink is too small to submerge your entire sheet pan, soak half the pan at a time or just put the cleaning ingredients right into your pan and let it soak.

- Using the rough side of a sponge or a scouring pad *(steel wool will scratch your pan)*, scrub like crazy in circular motions, getting into those corners and along the edges. You can also use a cleaning tool made especially for cleaning pans.

- Wash with hot soap and water to rid your pan of any remaining residue. Dry immediately to prevent rust from forming.

Before you can clean your pans, you have to get them messy. Let's get started...

Smoky Beef Nachos

1 lb. extra lean ground beef

2 tsp. garlic powder

1½ tsp. ground cumin

1 tsp. chipotle chile powder

½ tsp. salt

1½ tsp. cornstarch, divided

¼ C. water

¾ (12 oz.) bag multigrain tortilla chips

1 C. salsa con queso

1½ C. diced tomatoes

½ C. sliced green onions

1 or 2 jalapeño peppers, thinly sliced

Cilantro, sliced radishes, lime wedges, and sour cream for serving

Prep & Bake

Preheat the oven to 450° and line your sheet pan with foil. Crumble the beef onto the foil and sprinkle with the garlic powder, cumin, chile powder, salt, and ½ teaspoon of the cornstarch; mix to combine. Drizzle with the water and wrap the excess foil around the meat, sealing tightly. Bake for 20 minutes.

Open the foil packet carefully and stir. If the meat is still quite pink, return to the oven for a few minutes *(with the packet open)*. Remove the packet from the pan, drain the lilquid, and set aside.

Preheat your oven's broiler with the rack in the top position and carefully line the hot pan with foil *(parchment paper can be used, but don't let it extend over the edges, as paper near the heating element creates a fire hazard)*.

Arrange the chips on the prepped pan. Crumble the drained beef and arrange evenly over the chips; drizzle with the salsa con queso. Top evenly with the tomatoes, green onions, and jalapeños and broil a couple of minutes, until hot.

Finish

Sprinkle with cilantro and radishes and squeeze the juice from the lime wedges over the top. Serve with sour cream

Spicy Cajun Shrimp
& Sausage

1½ lbs. tiny potatoes

1 T. olive oil

½ C. butter, plus more for serving, melted

1 tsp. smoked paprika

½ tsp. ground cayenne pepper

½ tsp. dried thyme

½ tsp. salt

½ tsp. black pepper

½ tsp. garlic powder

4 ears sweet corn, cut into 2" chunks

1 lb. smoked Andouille sausage, sliced ¼" thick

1½ lbs. uncooked shrimp, peeled & deveined

Hot sauce and lemon wedges for serving

Parsley for garnish

Prep & Bake

Preheat the oven to 425° and grease or line your sheet pan. Put the potatoes on the prepped pan, drizzle with the oil, and toss to coat. Stir together ½ cup of the butter, the paprika, cayenne pepper, thyme, salt, black pepper, and garlic powder. Add the corn chunks to the pan and brush with a little of the seasoned butter; set the remaining butter mixture aside. Bake for 20 to 25 minutes.

Remove the pan from the oven and add the sausage and shrimp. Brush the remaining seasoned butter evenly over the food and bake an additional 10 to 15 minutes or until the shrimp is cooked and everything is heated through.

Finish

Serve with hot sauce, lemon wedges, and extra melted butter. Garnish as desired.

Serves 4

Cuban *Cha-Cha* Chicken

4 (6 to 8 oz.) skinless, boneless chicken breast fillets

1 lime, zested & juiced, divided

1 orange, zested & juiced, divided

¼ C. olive oil, divided

2 tsp. minced garlic

¼ C. chopped fresh oregano

1 tsp. ground cumin

½ tsp. ground cayenne pepper

Salt and black pepper

1 sweet onion

1 red bell pepper

1 orange, peeled

2 large Russet potatoes

Citrus Avocado Salsa, recipe on facing page

Prep & Bake

Preheat the oven to 425° and grease or line your sheet pan. Arrange the chicken on the pan and drizzle with the lime juice, 2 tablespoons of the orange juice, and 2 tablespoons of the oil; toss well to coat the chicken. Sprinkle both sides of the meat evenly the garlic, oregano, cumin, cayenne pepper, a big pinch each of salt and black pepper, and the zest of both the lime and the orange.

Slice the onion, bell pepper, and whole peeled orange into a bowl; cut each potato into six wedges and add to the bowl. Drizzle with the remaining 2 tablespoons oil and a pinch each of salt and black pepper and toss to coat; arrange around the chicken pieces in the pan, keeping the potatoes in a single layer. Bake for 40 to 45 minutes, drizzling with oil halfway through if needed, until the chicken is done (165°) and the potatoes are tender and golden.

While the food bakes, prepare the Citrus Avocado Salsa.

Finish

Serve chicken and vegetables with Citrus Avocado Salsa.

Citrus Avocado Salsa

Peel and dice 1 avocado and 1 orange and toss into a bowl. Seed and finely chop 1 jalapeño and add it to the bowl along with 1 C. chopped fresh cilantro, 1 T. orange juice, and a pinch of flaky sea salt; stir to combine.

Sprouts, Pancetta, 'Shrooms & Eggs

1½ lbs. Brussels sprouts, thinly sliced

2 leeks, halved lengthwise & thinly sliced

1½ T. olive oil, divided

Salt and black pepper to taste

4 oz. mushrooms, thinly sliced

2 garlic cloves, very thinly sliced

6 oz. pancetta or Canadian bacon, chopped

8 eggs

¼ tsp. crushed red pepper flakes

2 oz. crumbled feta cheese

Chives for garnish

Prep & Bake

Preheat the oven to 400° and grease or line your sheet pan. Toss the Brussels sprouts and leeks onto the prepped pan. Drizzle with 1 tablespoon of the oil and sprinkle with salt and black pepper; toss to coat. Arrange the mushrooms, garlic, and pancetta evenly over the top, drizzle with the remaining 1½ teaspoons oil, and bake about 10 minutes or until the sprouts are crisp-tender.

Remove the pan from the oven and create eight wells in the food. Crack one egg into each well and sprinkle eggs with pepper flakes, salt, and black pepper. Crumble the cheese over everything. Bake 10 minutes more or until the egg whites are set.

Finish

Garnish as desired.

BBQ Meatloaf Meal

1 to 1½ lbs. sweet potatoes

1 (12 oz.) pkg. frozen
   broccoli cuts *(don't thaw)*

¼ C. olive oil

1 tsp. seasoned salt

Salt and black pepper

1 lb. lean ground beef

2 eggs

¼ C. panko bread crumbs

¾ tsp. smoked paprika

¾ tsp. garlic powder

½ C. BBQ sauce, divided

Green onions for garnish

Prep & Bake

Preheat the oven to 400° and grease or line your sheet pan. Cut the sweet potatoes into ½" cubes and arrange them on one end of the pan; arrange the broccoli on the other end. Drizzle the oil evenly over the vegetables. Sprinkle the seasoned salt over the sweet potatoes and salt and black pepper to taste over the broccoli. Toss to coat, keeping the vegetables separate. Bake for 15 minutes.

Meanwhile, in a bowl, combine the ground beef, eggs, bread crumbs, smoked paprika, garlic powder, 1 teaspoon salt, and 2 tablespoons of the BBQ sauce. Mix with your hands until combined. Divide the mixture into four thick, oval patties, smoothing the edges. Arrange the patties in the center of the pan, leaving space between them.

Spread 1½ tablespoons of the remaining BBQ sauce over each of the patties and bake for 20 minutes or until the meat is done (160°) and the vegetables are tender.

Finish

Garnish as desired.

Tenderloin
with Roasted Veggies

2 T. olive oil

2½ T. honey

3½ T. balsamic vinegar

1½ tsp. minced garlic

1 tsp. black pepper

2 tsp. finely chopped fresh rosemary, divided

1 *(1 to 1¼ lb.)* pork tenderloin

3 C. halved Brussels sprouts *(quartered if large)*

2 parsnips, peeled & sliced ¼" thick

3 large carrots, sliced ¼" thick

1 red onion, cut into 8 wedges

Salt to taste

Prep & Bake

Preheat the oven to 425° and grease or line your sheet pan. In a small bowl, combine the oil, honey, vinegar, garlic, black pepper, and 1¾ teaspoons of the rosemary; whisk well.

Use paper towels to pat dry the tenderloin and set it on the prepped pan. Brush about 2 tablespoons of the oil mixture over all sides of the meat and sprinkle with the remaining ¼ teaspoon rosemary. Arrange the Brussels sprouts, parsnips, carrots, and onion around the meat and drizzle the remaining oil mixture over the vegetables; toss to coat and season with salt. Bake for 30 to 45 minutes or until the meat is cooked *(145°)* and the vegetables are crisp-tender.

Finish

Remove the pan from the oven, preheat the boiler, and set the pan under the heat for a few minutes to brown. Let the food rest for 5 minutes before slicing the meat.

Asiago Turkey
& Roasted Caesar

1 head cauliflower

Olive oil

Salt and black pepper
  to taste

1 garlic bulb

3 (6 to 7 oz.) turkey
  breast cutlets

⅓ C. grated Asiago cheese,
  plus more for serving

⅓ C. panko bread crumbs

1 T. chopped fresh parsley

1 romaine heart

Anchovy paste to taste

Worcestershire sauce
  to taste

Lemon wedges for serving

Prep & Bake

Preheat the oven to 450° and grease or line your sheet pan. Cut the cauliflower into florets and dump onto the prepped pan; drizzle with 2 tablespoons oil, toss to coat, arrange in a single layer, and sprinkle with salt and black pepper.

Remove the papery skin from the garlic bulb and cut off the top ¼", exposing the individual cloves. Set the garlic on foil large enough to wrap around the bulb; drizzle the cloves with oil, wrap the foil around the bulb, and set the bundle on the pan with the cauliflower. Bake for 30 minutes, stirring the cauliflower once or twice.

Drizzle a little oil over the cauliflower if it seems dry and move the florets to one side of the pan. Season turkey cutlets with salt and black pepper and arrange in the center of the pan.

In a bowl, combine the cheese, bread crumbs, parsley, 1½ tablespoons oil and a little salt and black pepper. Divide the mixture among the turkey cutlets and press gently to adhere; bake for 10 minutes, until the crumbs are golden.

Cut the romaine heart into three lengthwise wedges and arrange on the open side of the pan; drizzle with 1 tablespoon oil and season with salt and black pepper. Bake 5 minutes, until the turkey is cooked through *(165°)*, the cauliflower is tender, and the romaine has browned at the edges.

Finish

Spread some of the roasted garlic from the cloves over the food as desired, refrigerating any remaining garlic for another recipe. Spread anchovy paste over the romaine and drizzle with Worcestershire sauce. Squeeze the juice from the lemon wedges over everything. Serve with Asiago for sprinkling.

Chipotle-Lime
Shrimp Bake

1½ lbs. tiny red potatoes, halved

1 T. olive oil

¾ tsp. sea salt, divided

3 limes, halved

¼ C. unsalted butter, melted

1 tsp. ground chipotle pepper

½ lb. fresh asparagus

½ lb. broccoli or broccolini, broken into florets

1 lb. uncooked shrimp, peeled & deveined

Cilantro for garnish

Prep & Bake

Preheat the oven to 400° and grease or line your sheet pan. Toss the potatoes onto the prepped pan; drizzle with the oil, sprinkle with ¼ teaspoon of the sea salt, and toss to coat. Arrange in a single layer and bake for 30 minutes.

Meanwhile, squeeze juice from the limes to measure ⅓ cup; reserve the remaining fruit and those shells that have been squeezed. To the juice, add the butter, chipotle pepper, and the remaining ½ teaspoon sea salt.

Remove the pan from the oven and stir the potatoes. Arrange the asparagus, broccoli, shrimp, and all the reserved limes on top of the potatoes and pour the set-aside lime juice mixture evenly over everything. Bake 15 minutes or until the shrimp turn pink and the vegetables are tender.

Finish

Garnish as desired.

"Everything" Smoked Salmon *Egg Bake*

Note: Make sure your pan has at least 1" sides for this recipe.

Prep & Bake Preheat the oven to 300° and grease your sheet pan generously with coconut oil. In a big bowl, whisk together 16 eggs, ½ C. plus 2 T. milk, 2 T. chopped fresh dill, 1 tsp. salt, and ¼ tsp. black pepper and pour into the prepped pan. Cut grape tomatoes in half to measure 1 heaping cup. Drain and rinse 2 T. capers. Chop 4 oz. smoked salmon, thinly slice ½ red onion, and cut 4 oz. cream cheese into small pieces; distribute everything evenly over the eggs. Mix 1 tsp. poppyseed, ¾ tsp. dried minced onion, ¾ tsp. dried minced garlic, 1 tsp. black and/or white sesame seed, and 1 tsp. coarse sea salt and sprinkle evenly over the egg mixture. Bake for 25 minutes or until set.

Finish Cut into serving-size pieces.

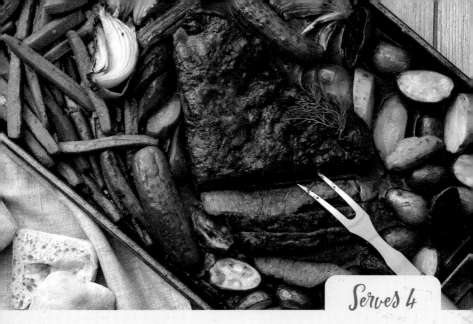

Quick Pickle Pot Roast

Prep & Bake Preheat the oven to 425° and grease or line your sheet pan. Cut 1 yellow onion into eight wedges and cut ¾ lb. tiny multi-colored potatoes in half; place on the prepped pan along with ½ lb. carrot sticks. Drizzle with 2 T. olive oil, toss to coat, and bake for 20 minutes. Stir together 1 (1.1 oz.) pkg. dry ranch dressing mix and 1 (.8 oz.) pkg. dry brown gravy mix and rub over all sides of a 1¼ lb. top sirloin steak *(sprinkle remaining dry ingredients over the vegetables if you'd like)*. Move the vegetables to the outside edges of the pan and set the steak in the center. Lay 4 whole dill pickles around the steak and drizzle the food with ¼ C. pickle brine. Bake for 18 minutes. Remove the pan from the oven and heat the broiler. Broil the food for several minutes, until the steak is nearly done to your liking. Remove the pan from the broiler, tent with foil, and let stand for 10 minutes.

Finish Slice the steak and pickles.

21

Honey-Pineapple Chicken Fajitas

2 T. coconut oil, melted

1 T. chili powder

2 tsp. ground cumin

1 tsp. garlic powder

1½ tsp. salt

2 T. honey

2 T. lime juice

1½ lbs. boneless, skinless chicken breasts, cut into bite-size pieces

1 sweet onion, sliced into half moons

2 red bell peppers, cut into strips

2 green bell peppers, cut into strips

1 (20 oz.) can pineapple chunks, drained

12 (6") corn or flour tortillas

Pico de gallo, sour cream, sliced jalapeño peppers, sliced avocado, and lime wedges for serving

Prep & Bake

Preheat the oven to 425° and grease or line your sheet pan. In a big bowl, whisk together the oil, chili powder, cumin, garlic powder, salt, honey, and lime juice. Add the chicken, onion, bell peppers, and pineapple and toss to coat. Dump the mixture onto the prepped pan in a single layer. Bake for 20 minutes.

Remove the pan from the oven and preheat your broiler. Broil for a few minutes, until the vegetables have lightly browned and the chicken is no longer pink.

Finish

Warm the tortillas, fill with chicken and vegetables, and top with pico de gallo, sour cream, jalapeño peppers, and avocado; squeeze juice from lime wedges over the food.

23

Serves 3

Sweet Curry Chops

Simple Yogurt Sauce, recipe on facing page

4 tsp. mild curry powder

1 tsp. black pepper

1 tsp. brown sugar

2½ tsp. salt

1 small head cauliflower

3 small sweet potatoes

3 (¾"- to 1"-thick) bone-in pork chops

2½ T. olive oil

Sliced radishes and parsley for garnish

Prep & Bake

Arrange an oven rack in the top third of the oven and preheat oven to 450°. Grease or line your sheet pan. Prepare the Simple Yogurt Sauce and refrigerate until needed.

In a small bowl, stir together the curry powder, black pepper, brown sugar, and salt; set aside.

Cut the cauliflower into florets and cut the sweet potatoes in half lengthwise *(if the sweet potatoes are large, cut into wedges)* and arrange on the prepped pan along with the pork chops. Drizzle the oil over the food, sprinkle with the curry mixture, and toss to coat.

Bake for 30 minutes or until the chops are cooked through *(145°)* and the vegetables are fork-tender and deep brown underneath. If the chops finish cooking before the sweet potatoes, remove them to a plate and cover with foil until the sweet potatoes are done.

Finish

Garnish as desired. Serve the food with the chilled Simple Yogurt Sauce.

Simple Yogurt Sauce

Whisk together ⅔ C. plain Greek yogurt, 1½ T. lemon juice, ¼ tsp. garlic powder, ½ tsp. salt, and a pinch of black pepper.

Garlicky Garden Tilapia

¼ C. unsalted butter, melted

4 garlic cloves, minced

2 T. lemon juice

1 tsp. Italian seasoning

1 lb. fresh asparagus

1½ C. cherry tomatoes

¼ C. olive oil, divided

Salt and black pepper to taste

4 (6 oz.) tilapia fillets, thawed if frozen

2 ciabatta rolls for serving, split

Parsley for garnish

Prep & Bake

Preheat the oven to 425° and grease or line your sheet pan. In a small bowl, whisk together the butter, garlic, lemon juice, and Italian seasoning; set aside 2 tablespoons of the mixture for the rolls.

Arrange the asparagus and tomatoes in a single layer in the prepped pan; drizzle with the oil, sprinkle with salt and black pepper, and toss to coat. Move the vegetables to the outside edges of the pan. Arrange the tilapia in the center of the pan and drizzle with the butter mixture. Bake for 10 minutes.

Spread the set-aside butter mixture evenly over the cut side of the rolls; set the rolls on a piece of foil and place gently on the vegetables. Bake a few minutes more, until the rolls are warm, the fish flakes easily with a fork, and the tomatoes begin to burst.

Finish

Garnish as desired.

Vegetable Chili
& Buttermilk Biscuits

3 T. vegetable oil
1 T. chili powder
½ tsp. ground cumin
1¾ tsp. salt, divided
1 head cauliflower
1 poblano chile pepper
4 green onions
¾ C. stone-ground cornmeal
½ C. flour
2 tsp. baking powder
1 T. brown sugar

¼ C. unsalted butter
⅔ C. buttermilk
⅔ C. shredded sharp
   cheddar cheese, divided,
   plus more for serving
1 (15 oz.) can black beans
1 (8 oz.) can tomato sauce
1¼ C. frozen sweet corn
   (don't thaw)
1½ C. vegetable broth
Parsley for garnish

Note: Make sure your pan has at least 1" sides for this recipe.

Prep & Bake

Preheat the broiler. In a big bowl, stir together the oil, chili powder, cumin, and ½ teaspoon salt. Cut the cauliflower into small florets, seed and dice the poblano, and chop the green onions; add the veggies to the oil mixture and stir to coat. Dump everything onto the prepped sheet pan, arrange in a single layer, and broil for 7 to 10 minutes, until brown around the edges.

Meanwhile, whisk together the cornmeal, flour, baking powder, brown sugar, and ¾ teaspoon salt. Cut the butter into cubes and work into the dry ingredients with your fingers until the mixture is crumbly. Add the buttermilk and ⅓ cup of the cheese, stirring with a fork until combined.

To the roasted vegetables, add the beans with their liquid, the tomato sauce, frozen corn, broth, and ½ teaspoon salt; stir gently. Scoop the biscuit dough on top of the veggie mixture in 12 mounds, leaving space between them. Sprinkle the dough evenly with the remaining ⅓ cup of the cheese. Bake for 25 to 30 minutes, until the chili starts bubbling and the biscuits turn golden brown.

Finish

Sprinkle with extra cheese and garnish as desired.

Serves 4

Turkey Fried Rice

Prep & Bake Preheat the oven to 400° and grease or line your sheet pan. Cut 1¼ lbs. boneless, skinless turkey breast into 1" cubes and place in a single layer on the prepped pan; season with salt and black pepper. Bake for 5 minutes. In a small bowl, whisk 2 eggs; pour onto the hot pan and bake 3 to 4 minutes, until the egg is cooked. Use a fork to break up the egg into tiny pieces. Drain 1 (15 oz.) can peas and carrots combo and coarsely chop ½ white onion; add to the hot pan along with 2 C. ready-to-eat rice. Drizzle ⅓ C. soy sauce and 3 T. sesame oil over the food, toss to coat, and arrange in a single layer; sprinkle with a few chopped green onions. Bake an additional 10 to 15 minutes or until the turkey is no longer pink.

Finish Toss rice mixture and drizzle with a little orange juice before serving.

Sausage & Greens

Prep & Bake Preheat the oven to 425° and grease or line your sheet pan. Crumble 1 lb. ground mild sausage onto one side of the prepped pan. Shred 2 medium sweet potatoes and spread out beside the sausage. Coarsely chop 1 orange bell pepper and ½ red onion and toss onto the sweet potato shreds. Pour 3 T. melted butter over the vegetables, toss to coat, and spread out evenly, leaving the sausage separate. Bake for 15 minutes. Sprinkle the vegetables with 1 T. of your favorite seasoning *(we used steak & chop seasoning)*. Remove and discard the thick stems from 1 bunch of kale and roughly chop the leaves; spread evenly over the vegetables. Crumble sausage again and layer on top of the kale; distribute the food to fill the pan. Bake about 3 minutes, until the kale just begins to wilt. Create eight wells in the food and crack an egg into each. Bake an additional 10 minutes or until egg whites are set.

Finish Season eggs to taste.

31

Gyro Meatball Pitas
with Citrus Potatoes

2½ lbs. Russet baking potatoes

1 lemon

1½ C. chicken stock

½ C. plus 1 T. olive oil, divided

7 garlic cloves, minced, divided

1 T. plus 1 tsp. dried oregano, divided

1½ tsp. sea salt, divided

½ lb. lean ground beef

½ lb. ground lamb or pork

¼ C. panko bread crumbs

2 T. chopped fresh parsley

3 T. grated onion

1 egg

½ tsp. ground coriander

½ tsp. ground cumin

¼ tsp. black pepper

2 oz. crumbled feta cheese

8 pita breads

Sliced cucumber, sliced tomato, plain Greek yogurt, and lemon wedges for serving

Prep & Bake

Preheat the oven to 400° and grease or line your sheet pan. Cut the potatoes into ½"-thick wedges and arrange on the prepped pan. Zest and juice the lemon. Measure ⅓ cup of the juice into a medium bowl; set the zest aside. Add stock, ½ cup of the oil, about ⅔ of the minced garlic, 1 tablespoon of the oregano, and 1 teaspoon of the sea salt to the bowl; stir to combine, pour over the potatoes, and toss to coat. Bake for 20 minutes. Flip the potatoes and bake 30 to 45 minutes longer or until much of the liquid is absorbed.

Meanwhile, in a big bowl, combine both types of meat, bread crumbs, parsley, onion, set-aside lemon zest, egg, coriander, cumin, black pepper, cheese, the remaining garlic, and the remaining ½ teaspoon sea salt. Blend gently with your hands until just mixed; divide into 20 equal-sized meatballs and set aside.

Discard the juices from the pan, wipe the pan dry, and drizzle the potatoes with the remaining 1 tablespoon oil. Move the potatoes to one side of the pan and place the meatballs on the other side. Bake an additional 15 to 20 minutes, until the meatballs are done (160°).

Finish

Warm the pita bread to soften, then fill with cucumber, tomato, meatballs, and yogurt. Serve the potatoes alongside the filled pitas and squeeze juice from the lemon wedges over the top.

Brown Sugar Chicken

2 small butternut squash, halved lengthwise & seeds removed

3 T. coconut oil, divided

2 to 3 T. maple pure syrup

¾ tsp. ground nutmeg

¾ tsp. ground cinnamon

1½ tsp. coarse salt

¼ C. brown sugar

4 chicken hindquarters

1 lb. cauliflower florets

1 tsp. garlic salt

Black pepper to taste

Parsley for garnish

Prep & Bake

Preheat the oven to 400° and grease or line your sheet pan. Set the squash halves on the prepped pan, cut sides up. Brush 1 tablespoon of the oil over the cut sides, drizzle with the maple syrup, and sprinkle with the nutmeg, cinnamon, and coarse salt.

Rub the brown sugar evenly into all sides of the chicken and arrange on the pan. Place the cauliflower on the pan, drizzle with the remaining 2 tablespoons oil, and sprinkle with garlic salt and black pepper; toss to coat and arrange in a single layer. Bake 30 to 40 minutes or until chicken is done (165°) and the squash and cauliflower are tender.

Finish

Remove the pan from the oven and heat the broiler. Broil the food for a few minutes until caramelized and lightly charred in places. Garnish as desired.

Serves 4

Blue Cheese Steak & Celery Bites *with Grapes*

Walnut-Blue Cheese
  Crumbles, recipe on
  facing page

Blue Cheese Butter, recipe
  on facing page

6 to 8 celery ribs

1 pt. cherry tomatoes

1 large bunch seedless red
  grapes

¼ C. olive oil

Salt and black pepper
  to taste

4 (6 to 8 oz.) boneless ribeye
  or New York strip steaks

Honey

Prep & Bake

Preheat the broiler and grease or line your sheet pan. Prepare the Walnut-Blue Cheese Crumbles and Blue Cheese Butter and set aside.

Cut each celery rib into 1" to 2" lengths and dump onto the prepped pan. Add the tomatoes and grapes beside the celery and drizzle everything with the oil; toss to coat, keeping everything separate. Arrange the celery pieces in a single layer at the edge of the pan, hollow side up. Sprinkle the tomatoes with a little salt and black pepper. Move the tomatoes and grapes to the outside edge of the pan.

Season both sides of the steaks with salt and black pepper and arrange in the center of the pan. Broil a few minutes on each side, until done to your liking, flipping once. If the grapes brown too quickly, remove them from the pan or lower the rack a bit.

Finish

Stuff the set-aside Walnut-Blue Cheese Crumbles into the hollows of the celery; drizzle with honey. Put pats of Blue Cheese Butter on the steaks, letting it melt into the meat.

Walnut-Blue Cheese Crumbles

In a small bowl, stir together 5 oz. crumbled blue cheese, ¼ C. finely chopped walnuts, ¼ C. chopped fresh parsley, and a bit of black pepper.

Blue Cheese Butter

In a small bowl, stir together 3 T. softened butter, 1½ T. crumbled blue cheese, and ½ tsp. chopped fresh thyme.

Mustard-Glazed Brats, Squash & *Kale Chips*

¼ C. olive oil

¼ C. spicy brown mustard

¼ C. apple cider vinegar

2 tsp. honey

½ tsp. salt

½ tsp. black pepper

1 (2 lb.) acorn squash, halved & sliced 1" thick, seeds discarded

5 uncooked brats

2 Granny Smith apples, cored & cut into 8 wedges each

4 C. coarsely chopped fresh kale *(packed)*

Prep & Bake

Preheat the oven to 425° and grease or line your sheet pan. In a bowl, whisk together the oil, mustard, vinegar, honey, salt, and black pepper. Arrange the squash, brats, and apples on the prepped pan. Remove 3 tablespoons of the mustard mixture from the bowl and brush it over the food; bake for 20 minutes.

Toss the kale with about 3 tablespoons of the remaining mustard mixture. Remove the pan from the oven and arrange the kale on top of the food. Bake 8 to 10 minutes more or until the kale is crisp, the brats are done *(160°)*, and the squash is tender.

Finish

Serve the remaining mustard mixture alongside the food.

Serves 4

Chops & Chickpeas

Prep & Bake Preheat the broiler and line your sheet pan. Chop the leaves from fresh rosemary sprigs until you have 1 teaspoonful *(reserve the stripped sprigs)*. On the prepped pan, combine 1 T. olive oil, the chopped rosemary, and the zest and juice from ½ lemon. Arrange 4 *(¾" thick)* center-cut bone-in pork chops on the pan, turning to coat both sides with the oil mixture; season generously with salt and black pepper. In a bowl, stir together 1 *(15 oz.)* can chickpeas *(drained & rinsed)*, 6 garlic cloves *(use roasted ones if you'd like, see pgs. 16-17)*, ½ C. sliced roasted red peppers, the stripped rosemary sprigs, 3 T. olive oil, and ½ tsp. each salt and black pepper and scatter around the chops; pour ⅓ C. chicken broth over the chickpeas. Broil 10 to 12 minutes, until the chops are cooked through *(145˚)*, basting several times and rotating the pan halfway through.

Finish Remove the stripped rosemary sprigs before serving.

40

Jumbo Chicken Pot Pie

Prep & Bake Thaw 1½ (17.3 oz.) pkgs. puff pastry
(3 sheets). Preheat the oven to 400° and grease or line your
sheet pan. Dump 1 (14 oz.) bag frozen pearl onions *(don't
thaw)* on the prepped pan. Shred 1 rotisserie chicken, thinly
slice 2 carrots and 2 celery ribs, and arrange everything in a
single layer on the pan; season generously with salt and black
pepper. Drizzle 2 (12 oz.) jars chicken gravy evenly over the
food. Stack two of the pastry sheets on top of each other on a
lightly floured work surface and roll out to 15x15"; cut into
1" strips. Fold the remaining pastry sheet in half and roll
out to 7x15", then cut into 1" strips. Arrange all the strips
crosswise over the filling, overlapping so most of the filling
is covered. Trim off any overhang from the sides of the pan.
Whisk an egg with a splash of water and brush over the pastry.
Bake 35 to 40 minutes, until the pastry is deep golden brown.

Finish Let stand 5 minutes before serving.

Mediterranean Trout

1 (2 lb.) trout fillet

1 lemon, thinly sliced

¼ red onion, thinly sliced

1 C. assorted olives

1 C. cherry tomatoes, halved

Several marinated sweet or hot peppers

1 T. capers

1 zucchini, sliced in half moons

1 yellow summer squash, sliced in half moons

¼ C. olive oil

Sea salt and coarse black pepper to taste

Whole peppercorns, optional

1 to 2 T. chopped fresh oregano, rosemary, sage and/or thyme, plus sprigs for garnish

2 T. butter, sliced

Prep & Bake

Preheat the oven to 425° and grease or line your sheet pan. Set the trout on the prepped pan, tucking the thin end under so it cooks evenly.

Arrange the lemon, onion, olives, tomatoes, peppers, capers, zucchini, and yellow squash on and around the trout. Drizzle the oil over everything and sprinkle with sea salt, black pepper, and chopped herbs. Scatter the butter evenly over the top. Bake for 20 to 30 minutes or until the trout flakes easily with a fork.

Finish

If you added them, remove the peppercorns before serving. Garnish as desired.

Cashew Chicken

⅓ C. soy sauce

1 T. hoisin sauce

1 T. apple cider vinegar

2 T. honey

1 tsp. toasted sesame oil

½ tsp. minced fresh ginger

2 tsp. minced garlic

2 T. cornstarch

½ C. water

1½ lbs. boneless, skinless chicken thighs

Salt and black pepper to taste

1 head broccoli

1 red bell pepper

1 green bell pepper

¾ C. roasted unsalted cashews

Toasted sesame seed* and sliced green onion

2 (8.8 oz.) pkgs. ready-to-eat brown rice & quinoa combo

Prep & Bake

Preheat the oven to 400° and grease or line your sheet pan. In a small saucepan over medium heat, whisk together the soy sauce, hoisin sauce, vinegar, honey, oil, ginger, garlic, cornstarch, and water until combined. Heat until the sauce thickens and bubbles, stirring often, then remove from the heat.

Cut the chicken into 1" cubes and toss onto the prepped pan; sprinkle with salt and black pepper and drizzle with half the sauce mixture, tossing to coat. Bake for 8 minutes.

Meanwhile, cut the broccoli into florets and cut the bell peppers into chunks. Add the vegetables and the cashews to the hot pan, season with salt and black pepper, drizzle with a little of the remaining sauce, and stir everything together. Bake about 20 minutes more, until the chicken is no longer pink.

Remove from the oven, drizzle with the remaining sauce, and sprinkle with toasted sesame seed and green onion.

Finish

Heat the brown rice & quinoa according to package directions, divide into serving bowls, and spoon the chicken and vegetable mixture over the top.

* To toast sesame seed, place in a dry skillet over medium heat about 6 minutes or until golden brown, stirring occasionally.

Rainbow Adobo
Portobello Tacos

1½ T. purchased adobo seasoning *(or make your own, recipe below)*

¾ lb. portobello mushrooms, sliced

½ to 1 red onion, sliced

1 red bell pepper, cut into strips

1 or 2 large carrots, cut into sticks

1 yellow summer squash, cut into strips

2 T. olive oil

Juice of 2 limes

Taco shells

Romaine lettuce leaves

Guacamole, black olives, diced tomatoes, and shredded Colby-Jack cheese for serving

Prep & Bake

Preheat the oven to 425° and grease or line your sheet pan. Prepare the Adobo Seasoning, if making, and set aside. Arrange the mushrooms, onion, bell pepper, carrots, and squash on the prepped pan and drizzle with the oil and lime juice. Sprinkle everything evenly with the adobo seasoning and bake for 15 minutes, until the vegetables are tender.

Finish

Fill taco shells with lettuce, mushrooms, and vegetables. Add guacamole, olives, tomatoes, and cheese.

Adobo Seasoning

Mix 2 T. salt, 1 T. paprika, 2 tsp. black pepper, 1½ tsp. each onion powder, dried oregano, and ground cumin, and 1 tsp. each garlic powder and chili powder. Keep in a sealed jar.

47

Serves 4

Lemon-Parm Chicken

1 egg

2 T. lemon juice

1½ tsp. chopped fresh parsley

4 tsp. minced garlic, divided

Salt and black pepper

4 boneless, skinless chicken breasts *(about 1¾ lbs.)*

½ C. dry bread crumbs

⅓ C. grated Parmesan cheese

1 lb. tiny yellow potatoes

1 lb. fresh green beans

½ C. butter

2 lemons, divided

Prep & Bake

In a shallow pan, whisk together the egg, lemon juice, parsley, 2 teaspoons of the garlic, and ½ teaspoon each salt and black pepper. Coat both sides of the chicken with the egg mixture, then let marinate for 30 minutes.

Preheat the oven to 400° and grease or line your sheet pan. On a plate, mix the bread crumbs and cheese. Dredge the chicken pieces in the bread crumb mixture, pressing lightly to coat evenly. Arrange on the prepped pan and spritz the top of the chicken pieces with cooking spray. Quarter the potatoes and arrange around one side of the chicken. Arrange the beans on the other side.

Melt the butter and mix with the remaining 2 teaspoons garlic, plus salt and black pepper to taste. Pour half the mixture over the potatoes and the other half over the beans; toss to coat and bake for 15 to 18 minutes.

Remove the pan from the oven and heat the broiler. Slice one of the lemons and add the slices to the pan. Broil the food for 10 minutes or until the chicken is done *(165°)* and the potatoes and beans are tender.

Finish

Cut the remaining lemon in half and squeeze some of its juice over the food.

49

Serves 4

Lingonberry Salmon

Prep & Bake Preheat the oven to 400° and grease or line your sheet pan. Lay 4 salmon fillets *(thawed if frozen)* down the center of the pan, skin side down. Cut 2 zucchini and 2 fennel bulbs in half lengthwise; cut the fennel into thin wedges and arrange the veggies around the outside of the pan. In a medium bowl, stir together 3 T. olive oil and 1½ tsp. fresh thyme leaves; drizzle evenly over the vegetables and toss to coat. Drizzle a little olive oil and lime juice over ½ lb. cherry tomatoes and add them to the empty area of the pan. Sprinkle everything generously with salt and coarse black pepper. Bake 15 to 17 minutes, until the salmon flakes easily and the vegetables are crisp-tender. Meanwhile, stir together ¼ C. lingonberry jam, 1 T. soy sauce, 1 T. lime juice, and a bit of cayenne pepper. Remove the food from the oven, but don't turn off the heat.

Finish Spoon the jam mixture over the salmon and return to the oven until the sauce bubbles.

Big Pan Jambalaya

Prep & Bake Preheat the oven to 425° and grease or line your sheet pan. Cut 12 mini bell peppers *(any color)* in half and thinly slice ½ (14 oz.) pkg. Polska kielbasa; toss onto the prepped pan. Drizzle with 2 T. olive oil and sprinkle with 1½ tsp. Creole seasoning. Bake for 8 minutes. Meanwhile, in a bowl, combine ¾ lb. medium uncooked shrimp *(peeled & deveined)*, 1 pt. cherry tomatoes *(halved)*, 1 T. olive oil, ¾ tsp. Creole seasoning, and ¾ tsp. paprika; toss to coat, add to the pan with the veggies, and stir gently. Bake for 7 minutes. Add 2 (8.8 oz.) pkgs. ready-to-eat rice *(or use 2 C. leftover steamed rice)*, ½ tsp. each salt and black pepper, and 1 tsp. Creole seasoning and toss to combine. Bake a few minutes longer, until the rice is heated through and the shrimp is done.

Finish Sprinkle with green onions.

Serves 6

Smoky Spinach
& Artichoke Pizza

1 T. cornmeal

1 C. warm water

1 (.25 oz.) pkg. active dry yeast

1 T. sugar

2½ C. flour, plus more for sprinkling

1 tsp. salt

¼ C. olive oil, divided

1 tsp. Italian seasoning

6 garlic cloves

1½ C. shredded smoked provolone cheese

1 (6 oz.) bag fresh baby spinach

2 (6.5 oz.) jars marinated artichoke hearts

Red pepper flakes to taste

Prep & Bake

Preheat the oven to 425° and sprinkle the cornmeal evenly on your sheet pan.

Pour the water into the bowl of a stand mixer and add the yeast and sugar. Let stand for 10 to 15 minutes until the yeast becomes frothy. Add 2½ cups flour and mix using the hook attachment. Add the salt and 2 tablespoons of the oil. Mix for 3 to 4 minutes, until the dough is firm. Let stand for 3 to 4 minutes.

Sprinkle a work surface and a rolling pin with a little flour. Roll the dough into a rectangle a little smaller than the prepped pan and carefully transfer the dough to the pan; stretch the dough to the corners. Spread 1 tablespoon of the remaining oil all over the top of the dough and sprinkle evenly with the Italian seasoning, garlic, and half the cheese.

In a bowl, mix the remaining 1 tablespoon oil with the spinach to coat; arrange evenly over the cheese. Drain the artichokes and arrange over the spinach; sprinkle with the remaining cheese and the pepper flakes. Bake for 12 to 15 minutes, until the cheese is bubbly and the crust is golden brown.

Finish

Cut into serving-size pieces.

Hasselback Ham
with Rutabaga "Fries"

2 lbs. boneless ham
6 slices Swiss cheese, halved
1 tsp. minced garlic
½ tsp. black pepper, divided
¼ C. butter, melted, divided
½ tsp. salt, divided

1 (1 lb.) rutabaga, cut into french fry shapes
1 lb. asparagus, halved
Honey
Chives for garnish
Grainy mustard for serving

Prep & Bake

Preheat the oven to 400°; grease your sheet pan, set a 12" square piece of foil in the center, and set the ham on the foil. Make 12 even cuts through the top of the ham, without cutting through the bottom; place ½ slice of cheese into each cut. In a big bowl, mix the garlic, ¼ teaspoon of the black pepper, and 2 tablespoons of the butter and brush all over the ham. Pull the foil up around the ham and cover tightly with more foil.

In the same bowl, stir together 1 tablespoon of the remaining butter, ¼ teaspoon salt, and the remaining ¼ teaspoon pepper. Add the rutabaga, toss to coat, and arrange in a single layer beside the ham. Bake for 45 minutes; flip fries over.

In the same bowl, combine the asparagus, the remaining 1 tablespoon butter, and the remaining ¼ teaspoon salt; toss to coat and arrange in the pan. Bake 12 to 15 minutes, until ham is heated through *(140°)* and vegetables are fork-tender.

Finish

Drizzle ham with honey, garnish as desired, and serve with mustard.

Serves 4

Chicken Bruschetta

⅓ C. balsamic vinegar

¼ C. olive oil

2 tsp. minced garlic

½ tsp. salt

½ tsp. black pepper

¼ tsp. dried oregano

¼ tsp. red pepper flakes

4 boneless, skinless chicken breasts *(about 1¾ lbs.)*

Bruschetta, recipe on facing page

¾ lb. tiny yellow potatoes

1 parsnip

1 yellow summer squash

A big handful of baby carrots

⅓ C. grated Parmesan cheese

Softened butter

8 small slices French bread

Basil for garnish

Prep & Bake

In a big shallow bowl, whisk together the vinegar, oil, garlic, salt, black pepper, oregano, and pepper flakes. Lay the chicken in the mixture, toss to coat, and marinate in the refrigerator for 1 hour. Meanwhile, make the Bruschetta and set aside until needed.

Preheat the oven to 425° and grease or line your sheet pan. Cut the potatoes in half. Cut the parsnip in half crosswise; cut the narrower end in half lengthwise and the wider end into four lengthwise slices. Cut the squash in half crosswise, then into lengthwise quarters. Arrange the cut-up vegetables and carrots in the pan in a single layer. Place the marinated chicken on top of the vegetables and pour the marinade evenly over everything. Bake for 20 minutes.

Spoon some of the pan juices over the chicken, then sprinkle the Parmesan evenly over the meat. Spoon about half the Bruschetta around the chicken. Butter the bread slices and lean against the rim of the pan. Bake an additional 20 to 25 minutes, until the chicken is done and bread is lightly toasted.

Finish

Serve the bread and the remaining Bruschetta alongside the chicken and vegetables. Garnish as desired.

Bruschetta

Stir together 2 C. quartered cherry tomatoes, 2 tsp. minced garlic, 3 T. chopped fresh basil, 2 tsp. olive oil, and salt and black pepper to taste.

Squash & Feta
Dinner Salad

1½ lbs. acorn squash, halved lengthwise, seeded & cut into ¼" slices

8 T. olive oil, divided

1½ tsp. coarse salt, divided

¼ tsp. coarse black pepper

4 C. cubed ciabatta bread

½ lb. block feta cheese, cut into ½" to 1" cubes

¼ C. red wine vinegar

1 tsp. honey

1 tsp. fresh thyme leaves

6 to 8 C. torn radicchio or endive or 2 (5 oz.) pkgs. mixed greens

Pumpkin seeds

Chopped Anaheim chile peppers

Prep & Bake

Arrange an oven rack in the top third of the oven and preheat oven to 400°. Grease or line your sheet pan.

Put the squash on the sheet pan and toss with 2 tablespoons of the oil, the black pepper and 1 teaspoon of the salt. Arrange in a single layer and bake 15 to 20 minutes, until squash just begins to brown around the edges; flip squash over and put the bread and cheese cubes over the top. Bake 15 to 20 minutes longer, until squash is tender and bread is toasted. Meanwhile, whisk together the vinegar, honey, thyme, the remaining 6 T. olive oil, and the remaining ½ tsp. salt; set aside.

Finish

Remove the pan from the oven and let stand 5 minutes. Pile radicchio or greens on the hot food, drizzle with the vinegar mixture, and toss to coat. Scatter pumpkin seeds and chile peppers on top. Serve immediately.

Big Sheet *Bacon & Browns*

Serves 6

Prep & Bake Preheat the oven to 400° and grease or line your sheet pan. Dump 1 (20 oz.) pkg. refrigerated hash browns onto the prepped pan and stir in ½ C. grated onion, 2 T. melted butter, 1 T. olive oil, 1 tsp. each garlic powder and paprika, plus salt and black pepper to taste; spread in an even layer and sprinkle with 1 C. shredded cheddar cheese. Bake for 15 minutes, until the edges begin to brown. Remove the pan from the oven and create six wells in the hash browns. Cut 6 bacon strips in half and line each well with two halves; crack an egg in the center of each. Sprinkle each egg with Parmesan, Romano, and/or Asiago cheese and season with salt and black pepper. Bake an additional 15 minutes or until the egg whites are set and the bacon is cooked. *NOTE: For crispier bacon, add it with the cheddar cheese so it bakes the entire time. Then add just the eggs to cook the last 15 minutes.*

Finish Garnish with parsley or chives.

Smoked Sausage
with Apples & Roots

Prep & Bake Preheat the oven to 400° and grease or line your sheet pan. In a big bowl, whisk together 2 T. olive oil, 2 T. Dijon mustard, 2 T. maple syrup, and ¾ tsp. fresh thyme leaves. Cut 1 (12 oz.) pkg. beef smoked sausage, 2 Honeycrisp apples, and 1 large sweet onion into 2" chunks and add to the bowl along with 1 lb. tiny yellow potatoes and ½ lb. petite carrots. Add 2 parsnips *(peeled and thinly sliced)*; toss to coat, dump onto the prepped pan in a single layer, and sprinkle generously with salt and black pepper. Lay several sage leaves on top of the food and bake for 50 minutes or until the vegetables are tender, stirring halfway through.

Finish Remove the sage leaves before serving.

Moroccan Chicken

¼ C. olive oil

2 T. honey

2 tsp. ground cumin

1 tsp. ground coriander

1 tsp. ground ginger

1 tsp. ground cayenne pepper or paprika

1 T. minced garlic

3 lbs. chicken pieces

1 red onion, quartered

1 lb. tiny red potatoes, halved

1¼ C. dried apricots

Cool Zhoug Sauce, recipe below

Coarsely chopped pistachios

Mint and cilantro for garnish

Prep & Bake

Preheat the oven to 350° and grease or line your sheet pan. In a small bowl, stir together the oil, honey, cumin, coriander, ginger, cayenne, and garlic. In a big bowl, combine the chicken, onion, and potatoes and drizzle with ¾ of the honey mixture; toss to coat. Arrange in a single layer in the prepped pan; bake for 35 minutes.

Toss the dried apricots with the remaining honey mixture. Add to the pan and bake 15 to 20 minutes longer, until the chicken is done (165°). Meanwhile, make the Cool Zhoug Sauce and set aside.

Finish

Sprinkle food with pistachios and garnish as desired. Serve with Cool Zhoug Sauce.

Cool Zhoug Sauce

Mix ¾ C. chopped cilantro, ½ C. chopped mint, ¼ tsp. each ground cumin and ginger, the zest and juice of 1 lime, ¼ C. olive oil, a little honey, and sea salt to taste.

Index

Meals

Finishing Touches